A REASON TO RETIRE

Suann Schuster

This book is dedicated to all of my friends and family entering the wild, wild, west of Retirement. Be gentle with yourselves, enjoying Life takes faith and practice. Hopefully we won't break….. until we're mulch.

TABLE OF CONTENTS

A REASON TO RETIRE

How We Got Here

We are the baby - boomer generation. We have been working, some of us, since our paper routes in the 1960's. For me that's over 50 years. We didn't make a lot of money, most of us, but we did have great adventures. Our retirement finances are a joke, and we can't afford to travel. Not a pot to piss in, as my momma used to say. So, when someone asks if we are going to retire, we can't imagine when, why or how.

I had been looking forward to no alarm clocks, no deadlines and no traffic for years but once I got here, in the wild west of Retirement it was quite a culture shock. Now there are no more stupid staff meetings, no more shitty bosses, no cleaning strangers bodily fluids and no more ass kissing, oh and no paperwork.

Did you know that nothing happens during the day. There is no entertainment until the evenings and by then I am tired from a long day of doing whatever the hell I want. When no one was around to tell me where to go I forgot to move for a while. The first few months were like living through Post Traumatic Stress Disorder.

I would awaken in a sweat thinking I was late for work. I would sleep till 11am and feel lost the rest of the day. It is the most unique and yet least understood time in our lives. Is it okay to watch Oprah? Do I have to leave the house everyday?

 I was quite surprised by the changing of seasons, time stands still some days and rushes by on others when we are paying attention. So many things we didn't notice over the years. Time, they say, is timey- whimey and it really does. Before retirement my hours flew by most days, filled with appointments, paperwork, traveling around the community every day. I went to bed each night calculating how much sleep

I could gather until the morning when every minute of the day raced before my eyes. I scheduled my time off and generally spent it catching up on work or maintaining my home. If I was lucky and motivated I might read a book, get time to read the Sunday paper, or maybe take a trip to the beach in summer. Mostly I stayed home, used my vacation to pay for bills and dreamt of luxurious vacations I would never take.

For many, many years we had <u>days,</u> and now we have <u>time.</u> Time for forgotten sun rises, soaking up some sun with a cup of Earl Grey, playing games and living one day at a time.

However you decide to spend your time each day is okay. We are some of the first individuals of our generation who are healthy enough to enjoy retirement.

I ask myself everyday, does this stimulate my muscles, my brain, my soul, and my desire for kindness, then that is a pretty good day.   Every day now, I wake up and think, ok, I am still alive, all of my parts move, oh wait, yea, okay, now let's go to Starbucks in my pajamas for Coffee.

We Worked So Damn Hard

If there was a way to make a dime, I did it despite my training or education. I worked like a dog, overtime, on-call, weekends, holiday, evenings for forty years and then I retired.

It isn't even all about the cost of retirement or imagining your income for fifteen or twenty years without employment. It is our identity. If you asked some of us who we are, we would say mechanic, jack of all trades, teacher, business manager, IT worker, retail salesperson, service or care-giver to describe who we are and what our lives have amounted to up till now.

Many others describe themselves as parents, partners, grandparents, sisters or brothers who worked some many years at this particular job.

As for me, I worked every crappy job you could imagine, drove an ice cream truck, worked fast food, did dishes in a college kitchen, delivered a lot of newspapers, folded icecream boxes ina factory,mopped floors in gross kitchens that stunk like fish, folded laundry at the holiday inn, worked in a radio station, started a food bank and a homeless shelter in a small town in

Pennsylvania, I rang the bells for the Salvation Army, was a therapeutic massage professional, worked as a teacher, wife, Child Welfare worker and a Mental Health professional.

Then one day everything felt heavy, mind numbing, soul sucking, humanity destroying minutia. The staff were bitchy, the clients unresponsive, the people around me started to sound like clones of each other.

With expressions like "it is what it is", " no problem", and blank stares, people with no questions or answers, I knew it was time to walk away. I realized later that I had let more of me go than I had intended.

<u>Time To Reflect</u>

We have free time, groceries, toilet paper, we only do laundry once a week and cooking for you and your spouse means a lot of wasted food and leftovers. Everything is different.

Then the house is quiet, it is just all of a sudden, the phone rings less, the groceries last too long, and that anxiety about being late, getting more done in a day than is humanly possible seems to fade away. There will still be days where your brain implodes with the possibilities and you lose the day playing old Albums, don't panic.   This is the natural progression of aging people in our country.

It is inevitable that life changes and it must. It is up to us though, to figure out what comes next. There are no rules about how to live your life after you retire. You can rock on the porch and watch the sun go down or you can go rock climbing.

What happens when those titles have all been fulfilled, the babies all grown and our bodies slowing down. We may even have the house paid off, or at least manageable payments. We need

to take a nap in order to stay up past 10pm, it seems moving through the rat race becomes too difficult.   That whole life that you once managed for 30 years or more has changed.

We are the first generation, we boomers, to retire before we die and yet we live way too long. Science has taken us into really old age.

So Change is not going to be easy, especially after decades of successes, challenges, and now a new identity; it will happen whether we are ready or not.

These folks are lovely and seem kind to me. They are free photo stock from the internet, but they are all of us.

Did I Do Enough

I wanted to make a difference in the world but I don't want to keep working. My plan is to figure out how to retire without losing my mind and my money and maybe it will help someone else.

So, I was climbing out of the pool the other day naked and wet and my toe caught on the cement.

As gravity and centrifugal force hurled me forward, quite unflatteringly, through the air, arms flailing, boobs in every direction, feet tangled, I grimaced in preparation of the pain to come, I accepted the inevitable.

As I lay in the mulch, wet and defeated I surveyed the possible damages to my body and my pride. Twisting my limbs, as I fell three feet in order to minimize the damages and avoid the garden mulch, I hit the ground with a whimper, stunned.

This is what being 63 feels like. Some days, I can snoopy dance to I-Tunes on and other days I can barely balance my broken down knees and worn away hips. So pride goeth before the fall and knowing this allows me to keep falling while I try to keep my boobs out of my eyes. Don't get me wrong, I am healthy as many of us will be when we need to retire.

I always wondered why older people or women of years exercised so damn much. Now I know it is to keep standing upright. I retired overweight, with bad eating habits and a propensity to help strangers whether they wanted it or not. I have lost about 50 pounds, eat healthy and exercise a little so that the next embarrassing fall only hurts my ego.

As for the unwanted advice, I had to realize that when no one paid me any longer for my opinion, I needed to keep it to myself, probably my greatest challenge.

As a young woman, I thought we would live forever. I was going to bring peace to all the world, live in a commune holding hands and singing freedom songs. I wanted to be free to see the world and fulfill all of my childhood and life's fantasies. The reality is that time just moved forward, as it does and forty years later, I can see the finish line of my life. It is not exactly as I planned but I doubt anyone's life is the same as the life we planned in our twelve year old minds.

 We were going to be rock stars and world travelers, we were going to be rich and famous and never eat liver and onions and cold beets again.

Most importantly, we were never, ever going to have grandma blue hair, smell funny like old people and holler at the neighborhood kids.

Today, my deodorant failed me in the supermarket and I caught a glimpse of chin hair in the frozen food door.

I hollered at a kid who dashed out in the street in front of my car, and when I stopped dying my hair it turned black and gray so I shaved it. Now, today I saw a smelly old lady with a beard and a bald head reflecting in the frozen food aisle and it was me.

I never forget though, no matter how old I feel, we are all in the same boat. Some of us are bitching about our aches and pains and the cost of prescription medication. Deriding politics and modern technology, pining that youth is wasted on the young. Now that I am old, there is a little waste but we don't have their redbull or energy.

Back In The Day

The 1960's were an empowering time for white men but not for women. My first job paid $ 4.00 an hour and by the time I retired from a professional, college educated career I made $ 12.00 an hour and this is over 40 years. So having money to retire was never really an option. I lived most of my dreams , saw much of America, worked in an adventurous career in Appalachia, did make a difference in my little world and never, ever, saw aging coming.

Then I remembered a time in my 30's when I worked at an ice cream factory. This 70 year old woman stood next to me on the conveyor line helping me fold boxes that the ice cream dropped into. She was bent over at the chest, had one hell of a smokers cough and told me how her husband had died last year. Her fingers were gnarled by arthritis and her hair a nest of beauty salon products gone by and frayed and torn sweaters.

She would talk at her lunch break between puffs of smoke that she had to care for her adult grandson who couldn't find a job. She opined about that bastard of a husband who left them in debt, whom she missed terribly. So, being a young, smart ass I asked her why she didn't retire. Having no idea what that would entail at 38, she took a long draw off her camel, held the smoke and exhaled with a wheeze, saying, " what for?"

Many times since I have heard friends and family tell me that they would not know what to do with themselves if they retired. One fella told me that there was nothing on tv, and nothing to do. I thought, I will be damned.

I lived this great life, growing up from an amazing generation of technological advances and huge cultural changes from our parents' generation to the 21st Century. Yet, no one was talking about what came next and I knew that many of us must be looking for a life vest.

When I wasn't working massive
overtime I maintained a garden,
walked in the woods, read when I could
and traveled a little. I think like most of
us, I always thought that the future
would take care of itself. I never really
got to see my parents and
grandparents age gracefully, my mom
had cancer and most of my family died
abruptly in their 60's. Now, here I am
60 with no game plan. I never was
able to save money as a social worker
because our pay bottomed out at
$30,000.00 a year. I took care of the
states' kids and never had my own. My
money did go a little farther than most
but my partner was ill for many of
those early working years and the
money kept us afloat.

My story may seem similar to many people we know. Retirement was something rich people considered because we baby boomers lived our lives and loves, fulfilling our dreams/ the sky was the limit. We never really vacationed or traveled much but we always made sure that we had a roof over our head, food and clothes while we were house poor. If your parents lived long enough to retire and my dad and his dad did not, they did it on the cheap. My parents lived this life everyday with seven kids and it seemed to be enough. We spent the summer months at the beach, eating hot dogs and potato salad till school started back.

Every need was met but we kids never had a dime to play with. We started working our paper routes and then fast food restaurants and then real careers but we had to work very early in our lives. My parents never talked about their retirement and other than a life insurance policy, there was no spare money to save.

My parents rarely sprang for the ice cream truck let alone a twenty dollar bill. My dad would bribe me to come home from college many years later by giving me a twenty.

How We Do It

Never once though in my early years did I ever imagine a time when I couldn't just go make money, just enough to get by. I don't think we really thought the day would come when we didn't have to work. I remember feeling real surprise when I gave my aunt a little money and she said, "How can you afford this?", I assured her that I could always just go make more. She had retired years earlier and struggled to enjoy her years without a bit of play money. That's not fair, I know but short of all of us living in a commune, I don't have the answer.

Need help
COPING
with stress?
The Employee Assistance Program provides a
full spectrum of services and resources to help
federal civilian employees deal with stressors in
both the workplace and at home at no cost.
1-800-222-0364
FOH4You.com

Many years later, while working as a civil servant, I realized that I would receive vacation pay, health insurance and a retirement account that the employer paid into, every single paycheck, for every hour I worked.

The kids today talk about "Adulting", this was my first clue that the mantra my dad repeated every night at dinner, "You just have to work hard until you get it", was here. I guess I had worked hard enough. There was never enough money because the more I made, the more I used, the more I needed. In 1980 everyone believed that investing was a great way to make smart money

It was dollars we spent, just a couple of bucks here or there and it would add up. It was, in my mind, a little savings account. I put my 401k to work back in those days, more than once but everytime I did the stock market would crash and take away most of my savings. That didn't seem to be right or worth the risk. Even back then I knew that the only way to make real money was to work odd jobs, a couple of jobs at a time, sort of like the food delivery folks today.

The difference though between then in the 80's and now the 20's, among other things is that a dozen eggs is $6.00 and so is milk, bread, fruit and vegetables.

A young woman I know, an Osteo Assistant - joints and bones, currently makes about $27,000 a year and needs a part-time job. That 27K was about equal to my $13,000 in 1986 and it didn't buy much then. A one bedroom apartment can cost around $1200.00 a month. Our rent in 1983, in the same area, was $475.00 a month. We never thought we would make enough to buy a house.

 Give a person a fish and they will eat for a day. Teach one to fish and one day, hopefully they'll get to retire. So pay a fortune for an education or back in the day learn while you work and get paid the least.

When I would switch jobs I would need that odd job, rainy day money for car repairs or utilities and groceries. This poor woman could be living paycheck to paycheck.

When my tax return would come in each year it was an exciting opportunity for a few day trips or a new household appliance. If it really was much, or we let the Government take more each pay, maybe we could pay a little extra on our student loans, or car loans, or computer purchase loans, or my favorite……(name changed to protect me) rhymes with winger-nut. Evil and tempting and expensive.

I didn't even know anyone who had money stashed away for retirement. After my dad died, my mom went back to work and started a change jar. It was a huge wine making jug that she filled with quarters.

  Those funds gave her trips to Florida,
New York City, Vermont, and eventually
a big bash at her funeral. She
managed through work, help from my
brother, a social security check of a few
hundred dollars a month and wing and
a prayer. I could never help her keep
afloat because I was usually neck deep
in debt.

When I finally reduced my work hours
and took on a less demanding job I wa
in my 60's. I knew, like many of us
who grew up in the 1960's, that I really
had to figure out how to live out my life
without sleeping in a box on the
street.

Then one day I thought, I will just buy
everything I could ever need for
retirement, pay it off and then use my

social security to float me through to the grave. I paid off the house, landscaped the property, stock piled groceries, because that is what our parents did, and hunkered down. I started paying off all of our credit, and bought my car outright.

Well, that was all good for a few years but as the supplies dwindled and my body couldn't keep up with all the physical demands of daily life, I once again, had to reevaluate my plan. With no more grand dreams in my future that I could afford it was time to rethink aging.

A Plan

I needed a plan. What did I like to do when I had time to do whatever the hell I wanted? It was so, so long ago. I walked the twenty blocks between Canton St. and Niagara St. as a kid smoking a stolen cigarette and listening to my walkman radio, rode my bike, read, gardened, studied, enjoyed paint by number pictures or coloring.

I helped out my brothers with stacking wood and cleaning restaurants.   I loved driving, it was the most freeing experience back in 1976. I played guitar poorly and I loved to sing.

I tap danced and studied Karate, was in the Military, sang on-stage, and on and on walking with one foot in front of the other, jumping at most opportunities. Now I just wasn't motivated to look for opportunities.   ok, I'm rested, so what do I do with myself now? While working all those years, I also volunteered to wrap presents, and volunteered in the food banks, rang the Salvation Army bells, all with the little free time I had each week and now well-intentioned folks suggest that I volunteer.

European countries provide a month of paid vacation each year. In that culture everyone is encouraged to enjoy life, down time and to learn to rest throughout one's life.

In all those ridiculous hours I worked I had ten days vacation for the year and That has to change if we ever want to recover and transition from always tiring to retiring.   I never took a real vacation, I couldn't afford it. Returning to work after a week of rest was deceiving because before I was unpacked I would be behind at work . I accrued lots of overtime. I did travel a bit but each time we saved for months and scrimped in order to fly. It was expensive and stressful and really not worth the jet lag. The credit card debt makes taking a vacation akin to buying a car with down payments and maintenance.

 Most of the time while working, I took work home just to lighten the load. Don't get me wrong, in my 30's I could not be stopped. Now I am 63 and have to stop to pee.

What the hell, now my body is beat, my knees are always in rehab, I can't drive at night and now it's time for surgery after surgery just to put one foot in front of the other.

So this is what I have figured out in the last few years. I use a small app called STASH to invest in all sorts of companies, with $20.00 a month, it's a start. Next, I started my social security so I could stash it while I still worked a little. I opened my backyard pool by selling my first born, lol, and I swim for three months out of the year. I began crocheting again, an old skill that helped me connect with clients in the mental health system. I did as I said, bought my car outright and ten years later it runs well. I have a little hobbit house in a small town where I garden.

 I have been studying the German language and I am learning to play the piano. The one thing I never get used to is attending funerals but as long as I keep my ass moving and my brain sharp.

<u>The First step</u> - clean up your act, take a look at your life and reflect on what you want from your retirement. It will change and that's okay, it is just for now.

<u>Step 2</u> - Take stock now of how much money you have or can make in the next six months. You may live to be 100 or 65, who knows, so look at your current lifestyle and groom. Do I need to exercise or lose weight or quit smoking to live a better quality life. Pay down the bills you can and set a date for changing daily habits. It will be your new job.

<u>Step 3</u> - Develop a daily routine, if you want, that includes house chores, movement, and something, one activity, could be bungee jumping or bridge club, or gardening. Maybe it's as simple as getting up at the same time every day. When weather permits, I sit in the yard with a cup of tea and meditate and stretch. This routine or any focus will help you to adjust to your new world.

It is important not to make the same mistakes I did and pack too much expectation into each day or week, slowing down is okay, you are no longer a rat in the race. When you're mind starts to slow down, start a daily crossword, or Suduko, or play scrabble. The only way to keep young is to keep your mind active and your body healthy.

Step 4 - Notice the small things around you, changing seasons, the trees and birds. Try telling the time each day by the sun and sit in the grass. These activities will remind you, ground you to the world around you that really hasn't changed much since you were a kid. The sun still rises in the East and sets in the West. If this one sounds silly, trust me, lots of folks around you will want to fill your time with child care, volunteering, part-time employment so "you can get out more", don't fall for it. No one who is still working and running can understand what it's like to stop running.

Step 5 - This step worked well for me so give it a try. I paid off some bills while I was in the planning stages of retirement. Then make some long-term purchases like owning your new car, paying down the mortgage, fixing the house. Don't spend a fortune, just put a couple of hundred dollars you would spend on a night out on your future.

When I look back now, owning my car, and paying the mortgage down gave me the breathing room I needed to stop the panic in my head that "how will I live without a job". Between 401 k's if you have one, social security, and the last few months of the job you are soon retiring from forgo Christmas presents to the adult kids and set that aside.

https://www.stash.com

 I enjoyed STASH, a small investment company that allows me to deposit really small amounts of money that will grow a little. I mean really small, 1.00 if you want. Some stocks give dividends but considering all the money the stock market took from my 401K over the years, why not? When the day comes you will retire with a sense of relief but also peace because you made plans that didn't just take money.

What's Next

So at this stage of life, the Educational Psychologist Eric Erikson, writing about the stages of development described our senior years with " generativity vs. despair".

https://www.healthline.com/health/parenting/erikson-stages

We need to feel useful, valued or contributing or we can drift into sadness, apathy, and illness.

 We are in a mysterious place where no one knows how to be a "senior" and no one talks about it. We are men and women who didn't make enough money to avoid worrying about old age.

By the time we realized we were getting older, it was time to retire. We have a part-time job somewhere, we volunteer, give back to society, we care for our aging family and we stash a little money away. Our money is not s[e] secure or maybe just a little and we still have to fill our remaining days with some joy, forging ahead on our own.

When i was a bored kid I'd whine and drag my butt around the house, those late summers and holidays breaks seemed endless. My mom would tell us to "entertain ourselves" or she would find something for us to do. So as i try to maneuver through "I can do whatever the hell I want", those past busy morning routines and alarm clocks happen rarely. So now, if I get up around 11ish, and if I feel like waking and baking it is okay too, I just get a nap. That is such a foreign experience by comparison. No one talks about how hard it is to adjust to living in the moment, first I took a big breath, then I panicked, next I made myself as busy as I could possibly be.

One morning though after this self imposed retirement grieving, I sat on the back porch and soaked up the warm morning sun. After sipping a large glass of green tea I sat in the grass beneath my feet and hand pulled weeds while listening to music. That day lasted forever. I was calm, let my mind wander and when I couldn't sit still, I puttered, read and went for a walk. If you can outlast that initial freak out about money, time, FOMO - fear of missing out, retirement is the greatest joy.

 We are in culture shock with no internet support, or any comparable writing since my mother read Erma Bombeck. The only advertising I notice refers to Old people housing and those ads are horrid. You start seeing really bad actors from the 70's show up with their schtick to remind us our time is limited. Or the ads that assume all people over 55 are ill and really need a saving of 20% off wholesale urine tubes. Aging, memory loss, hearing loss, bladder loss, cheap coffee and the occasional discount seems to be our future. Although eating dinner earlier actually is great.

I don't think one type of retirement fits everybody. We social service retirees have to eek out a different way to slow down and enjoy life. That's where I'm stuck.

My new labels are the nosy Aunt, that lady who gives advice no one wants, the person always collecting money for some cause. Mostly, I am considered the relative who has everything and never leaves the house. We just want to rest, learn to play an instrument, write a book, or spend long hours at the library.

All the things that non-workaholics did when they were younger, concerts, vacations, parties, many of us never had the money, time off or opportunity to play. I looked at centers that give folks activities during the day:

Oh, here's a good one: we wandered downtown from the little park we live near, to the Senior Center.

There are still places in the world that are stuck in the 1950's and little town Senior Centers provide lunch and play cards. The floors were bare, no rugs in sight, card tables and metal chairs with one or two folks sitting at them. This place, a supposed haven and community center was a depressing, cold room with no art and no comfort.

We went to the next town over, with a larger population and a short drive and what a difference. This Senior Center had physical and social activities and opportunities to learn new skills. It brought a tear to my eye, thank god it smells nice here and artists teach the activities.

You can learn a language, join a pickleball team, whatever the hell that is, chat, play a game, crochet, paint, study computer coding, play cards, join the band, or sit in the lovely grassy knoll, off the edge of a park and visit.

With a small plan worked out now I just need the motivation to get there. When I looked around to see what I might want to do, there was the gym, movie theaters, shopping, going to lunch all of which became boring very quickly.

Now, library's are a joy, quiet, musty smell of book bindings and women our age wandering about shushing everybody. Some things never change. I listen to music, read anything I want including magazines and even audiobooks. The library is the last safe place for kids and ole folks.

Never Ending

I want the world to know that we have
experiences that are truly amazing.
We have learned some lessons no one
would want to repeat. We've lived
through poverty, and plenty.   Maybe a
we light the way we will inspire others.
Our current generation of children just
think old people are cute or sweet or
quaint. We aren't asked to talk about
our lives and most people think that
older folks have nothing to offer. It
does piss me off but I am still thrilled
the kids notice, we are not yet
invisible.

We were the original gangsters, O.G. born of the 60's sliding into the empowering 80's. Some of us put the greased lightning into the 70's and slid right into retirement with great routines and daily joys. Those folks were able to plan, and save while they lived. But, the vast majority of hundreds of thousands of seniors, we could never save a dime.

 To all of you who still have to work, never being able to retire, thank you for the trail-blazing freedom you built and sacrificed. Some of you are raising someone elses' kids or your grandkids, working double shifts and overtime so you can take a cruise in two years, working in a factory just to pay the rent, some are caring for fading loved ones or yourself as you fade.

There is a place a few minutes a day for worry, feeling old, complaining about the aches, feeling memories, we call it Putzing or German Putzen, cleaning mainly my mind. the rest of the time we try Yoga, scrapbooking, bocce or pickle ball, learn to play the piano, take week long trips w/ the girlfriends travel by bus, read Steven King or Siddharta or learn to rollerblade, I don't know what you would do, you amazing O.G, you do you, but please DO.

There isn't enough time left for being embarrassed, feeling inadequate, worrying about looking foolish, just live now as if you hadn't worked the last 40 years of soul sucking bedlam.

Some of us may want to fade away gardening in the backyard, get away from the world and that is okay too, for a little while. Spending too much time in the alone zone starts to shade your perspectives, opinions, and relationships. Take your time with your recovery but don't stay too long. The world still needs you.

The first half of our story made sense. We built lives, had children, worked all week and rested on the weekends ot not. We saved a little money, we spent a little money a few times a year for holidays and vacations. The idea was that once we "retired" we could slow down a bit. Think about our grandparents. Now this is just my North eastern, white, religious, third generation (German) American family. My grandfather died when I was six ,

{1964} and he was 66. He worked at his furniture business until he died. My maternal grandfather died when i was 12, he was a Pharmacist and took care of his wife, grandma Gracie, who was disabled from a stroke. My paternal grandma Schuster died when she was 94 and I 34. Everyday she prayed the full rosary several times, ate half a banana every day, visited sick friends, went to mass, and spent time with her children.

Now it is 2023 and I am 63. There are few examples of women in our society who have found some way to survive all "This retirement fun". No offense to my grandma but I want more. My mom did get to do a little travel and find a little joy but I know she struggled too. I want to enjoy this time in my life but with few living guides and the strange ways the body starts to betray you it is a difficult task. All of a sudden I can't cut the back and front lawn in the same day, I no longer have balance on a bicycle, have trouble seeing while driving at night, and sometimes I just need to sit down and rest. It has taken me several years to understand my body and what she may need to maintain physical and mental health. Be patient with yourself. Life, family, and work were pretty difficult periods in our lives. Remember, and this is important, you amazing O.G, (original gangster) you - do - you. You can tackle anything. More to come, I'll keep ya posted.